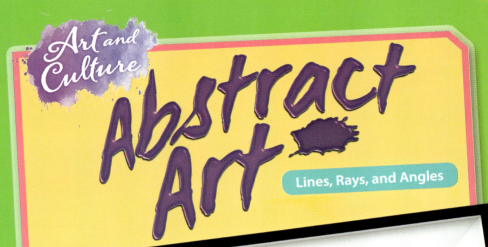

Art and Culture
Abstract Art
Lines, Rays, and Angles

Saskia Lacey

Consultants

Michele Ogden, Ed.D
Principal
Irvine Unified School District

Colleen Pollitt, M.A.Ed.
Math Support Teacher
Howard County Public Schools

Publishing Credits

Rachelle Cracchiolo, M.S.Ed., *Publisher*
Conni Medina, M.A.Ed., *Managing Editor*
Dona Herweck Rice, *Series Developer*
Emily R. Smith, M.A.Ed., *Series Developer*
Diana Kenney, M.A.Ed., NBCT, *Content Director*
Stacy Monsman, M.A., *Editor*
Kevin Panter, *Graphic Designer*

Image Credits: pp. 2–3 Thierry Gachon/ZUMA Press/Newscom; p. 4 Ian Dagnall/Alamy Stock Photo; p. 5 (top) DeAgostini/Getty Images; p. 6 The Print Collector Heritage Images/Newscom; p. 7 Vova Pomortzeff/Alamy Stock Photo; p. 8 Leemage/Corbis via Getty Images;
p. 9 Photo12/UIG via Getty Images; p. 10 Fine Art Images Heritage Images/Newscom; p. 11 akg-images/André Held/Newscom; p. 12 akg-images akg images/Newscom; p. 13 Universal History Archive/UIG via Getty Images; pp. 14–15 PA Images/Alamy Stock Photo; p. 15 (front) Moderna Museet; p. 16 (artwork) Peter Horree/Alamy Stock Photo, (portrait) David Gahr/Getty Images; p. 17 Jim Lo Scalzo/EPA/Newscom; p. 18 Crane Kalman, London/Bridgeman Images; p. 19 Christie's Images/Bridgeman Images; p. 20 (top) Private Collection/Bridgeman Images, (bottom) Christie's Images/Bridgeman Images;
pp. 20–21 dpa picture alliance archive/Alamy Stock Photo; p. 21 Active Museum/Alamy Stock Photo; p. 22 (bottom) Martha Holmes/The LIFE Picture Collection/Getty Images; pp. 22–23 Carl Court/Getty Images; p. 24 (bottom) Gordon Parks/The LIFE Picture Collection/Getty Images; pp. 24–25 B Christopher/Alamy Stock Photo;
pp. 26, 27 (front) Chance Yeh/Getty Images; p.27 (back) Mick Tsikas/Reuters/Newscom; all other images from iStock and/or Shutterstock.

Library of Congress Cataloging-in-Publication Data

Names: Lacey, Saskia, author.
Title: Art and culture. Abstract art / Saskia Lacey.
Description: Huntington Beach, CA : Teacher Created Materials, 2017. | Includes index. | Audience: Grades 4 to 6.
Identifiers: LCCN 2017012265 (print) | LCCN 2017012800 (ebook) | ISBN 9781480759459 (eBook) | ISBN 9781425855635 (pbk.)
Subjects: LCSH: Art, Abstract–Juvenile literature.
Classification: LCC N6490 (ebook) | LCC N6490 .L225 2017 (print) | DDC 709.04/052–dc23
LC record available at https://lccn.loc.gov/2017012265

Teacher Created Materials

5301 Oceanus Drive
Huntington Beach, CA 92649-1030
http://www.tcmpub.com

ISBN 978-1-4258-5563-5

© 2018 Teacher Created Materials, Inc.
Printed in China
Nordica.032020.CA22000029

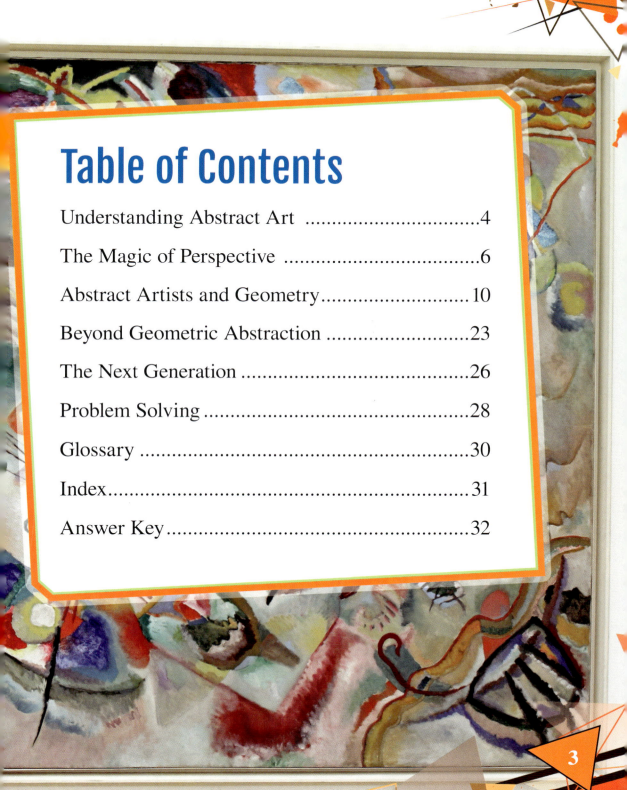

Table of Contents

Understanding Abstract Art 4

The Magic of Perspective 6

Abstract Artists and Geometry..........................10

Beyond Geometric Abstraction 23

The Next Generation 26

Problem Solving 28

Glossary 30

Index..31

Answer Key...32

Understanding Abstract Art

Many artists try to recreate what they see in the real world. They sketch landscapes or draw portraits of friends. They paint familiar objects. But, there are other artists who do not try to reflect the outside world. Their drawings, paintings, and sculptures serve a different purpose. These creators are known as abstract artists.

Wassily Kandinsky painted *Improvisation: Dreamy* in 1913.

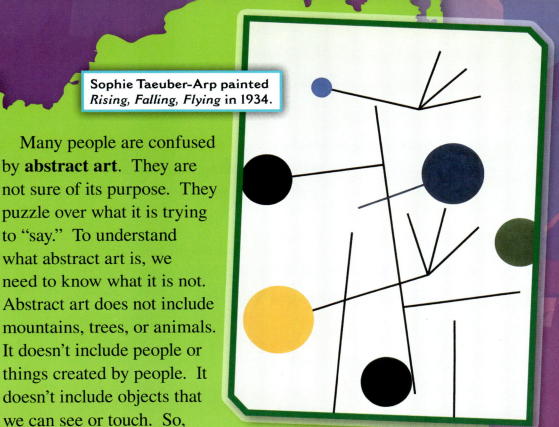

Sophie Taeuber-Arp painted *Rising, Falling, Flying* in 1934.

Many people are confused by **abstract art**. They are not sure of its purpose. They puzzle over what it is trying to "say." To understand what abstract art is, we need to know what it is not. Abstract art does not include mountains, trees, or animals. It doesn't include people or things created by people. It doesn't include objects that we can see or touch. So, what's left?

Abstract art features shapes, lines, and colors that do not resemble the real world. Instead, these works of art seek to create a feeling, mood, or idea. Artists like Wassily Kandinsky, Josef Albers, and Sophie Taeuber-Arp (TOY-ber-arp) were pioneers of abstract art. Their work changed the art world forever.

The Magic of Perspective

To truly grasp abstract art, we must explore how art has **evolved**. Before the era of the abstract, painters wanted to create realistic art. They tried to make their works as true to life as they could.

If you've ever tried painting, you might think this is a challenge. You start painting with high hopes. But then, you become frustrated. It doesn't look the way you thought it would. Many artists use the rules of **perspective** to help them overcome this challenge. Perspective helps artists create works that appear three-dimensional.

Before artists learned the rules of perspective, their paintings looked two-dimensional, or flat. A work like *Court of King's Bench* is an example of a painting that does not use perspective. There is no element of depth. So, the people in the drawing look the same size.

Court of King's Bench does not use perspective.

Visitors admire the perspective in this Raphael Sanzio painting.

As centuries passed, paintings became more and more lifelike. Some paintings almost seemed like photographs. These works took a *long* time to create. Artists put thought into every brushstroke. Raphael Sanzio used perspective in his paintings to make them look realistic. The people in the foreground look closer than the people in the background.

Impressionism

There was a great shift in the nineteenth century. A new group of painters arrived. They had a unique vision. They were called impressionists. Unlike earlier artists, they were not concerned with art that looked *exactly* like the real world. They were more interested in capturing the light and color of the moment. They painted quickly and often outdoors. Take, for instance, Claude Monet's *Water Lilies*. The painting shows real objects—water lilies. But, it is not a perfect representation. The painting could never be mistaken for a photograph. It is too abstract. The impressionists took the first step toward abstract art.

Water Lilies by Claude Monet

Three Musicians by Pablo Picasso

Cubism

After the impressionists, artists such as Pablo Picasso and Georges Braque (jawrj brahk) arrived. Their works were even more abstract. They were known as cubists. Cubists use geometric shapes to create their masterpieces. A great example of cubism is Picasso's *Three Musicians*. At first, the shapes stand out. There are squares and triangles. There are lines and circles. But, take a longer look. The shapes form three distinct figures. Picasso, like other cubists, painted objects from the real world. *Three Musicians* may seem strange. But, it is not purely abstract.

Abstract Artists and Geometry

Abstract art continued to grow in popularity. The first abstract works were geometrical. They were collections of expressive colors and shapes. Artists such as Kandinsky, Klint, Albers, Bauer, and Taeuber-Arp helped mold abstract art. Their works may seem simple. But, they often hide deeper meaning.

Wassily Kandinsky

Wassily Kandinsky is thought by many to be the first abstract artist. He was born in Moscow, Russia, in 1866. He came from a wealthy family. During his childhood, the painter traveled with his parents all over Europe.

Kandinsky painted in his youth. But, he moved away from art as an adult. He was worried about living an artist's life. He wasn't sure whether he would be successful. So, despite his love for painting, he completed a degree in law. But at the age of 30, Kandinsky had a change of heart. He decided to take a leap of faith. He would give up his career for the life of an artist.

Wassily Kandinsky

Black Spot by **Wassily Kandinsky**

LET'S EXPLORE MATH

Kandinsky's abstract works often include **points**, **lines**, **rays**, and **line segments**. Find examples of points, lines, rays, and line segments in the Kandinsky painting above.

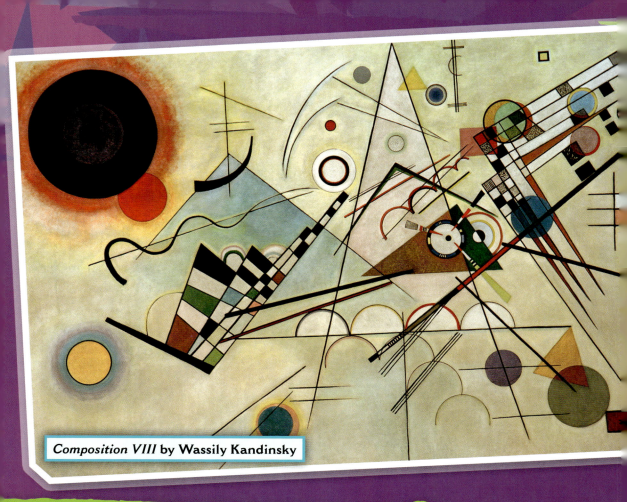

Composition VIII by Wassily Kandinsky

Kandinsky looked up to the impressionists. He respected the cubists. He was a great lover of art and art history. But, he also longed to do something different. He wanted to make art without a subject. He wanted his colors, lines, and shapes to speak for themselves. In this way, colors and shapes would become his language. They would express his feelings and emotions.

Every color had a different effect for Kandinsky. Each held a unique message. He even believed that colors had distinct sounds. He thought of yellow as a trumpet. The color blue was a pipe organ. This influence of music is clearly seen in Kandinsky's works. His *Composition VIII* seems to contain a symphony. Each of its brushstrokes sings like a note of music.

Kandinsky taught design and painting classes at an art school in Germany. Teaching helped him develop new ideas for future artwork. He also wrote two books during this time. His books explained the use of geometric shapes in his art. They are still popular today.

LET'S EXPLORE MATH

Kandinsky often included triangles in his paintings. The triangles have **acute**, **obtuse**, and **right** angles. The triangles can also be classified as **equilateral**, **isosceles**, or **scalene** based on the lengths of their sides.

1. Look at the triangles in Kandinsky's painting. Determine whether each angle is acute, obtuse, or right.
2. How do you know whether a triangle is equilateral, isosceles, or scalene?

Triangles in a Curve by Wassily Kandinsky

Hilma af Klint

Hilma af Klint is a lesser-known abstract artist. But, she is no less influential to the art movement. Her first works date before those of her more famous peers. Some scholars believe she, not Kandinsky, was the first true abstract artist!

Klint was born in Stockholm, Sweden. As a young woman, she attended art school. At the time, Klint was well known for landscapes and portraits. She kept her abstract art private. She didn't think that people would understand her work.

A gallery visitor views Klint's *Group IV, The Ten Largest* collection from 1907.

Over the course of Klint's life, she created hundreds of abstract wonders. She painted quickly, often creating several paintings a week. In her work, Klint reached for something beyond the physical world. She sought to connect with the spiritual realm. And, although Klint was small in stature, she created gigantic paintings. Some of them are over 10 feet (3 meters) tall!

Before Klint died, she made a decision. It would affect her legacy, or lack thereof, for many years. In her will, she ordered that her work not be made public for at least 20 years after her death. Her wish was granted. Her paintings weren't publicly shown until 1986—42 years after her death!

Hilma af Klint

Study for Homage to the Square by Josef Albers

Josef Albers

Josef Albers

The art of Josef Albers can be found in museums around the world. Albers was a German innovator. He invented new forms of art. One art movement was called op art. It focused on optical illusions. That's when the eye is tricked into seeing something that isn't there.

Like Kandinsky, Albers was a teacher. Albers taught at a school called Bauhaus for 10 years. His time as a teacher helped spark some of his brightest ideas. Albers once wrote, "A color has many faces, and one color can be made to appear as two different colors." Colors are very important in abstract art. Albers used color exercises to teach his students. They helped students study how colors interact.

One of Albers's great talents was creating illusions with color. He studied the way colors change. *Homage to the Square* is his most famous series. It studies how colors interact with one another. Each painting features a group of overlapping squares.

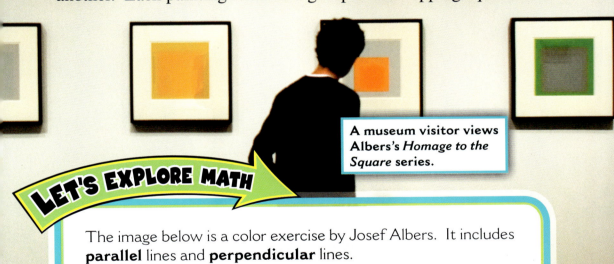

A museum visitor views Albers's *Homage to the Square* series.

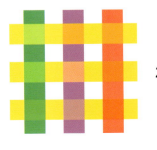

LET'S EXPLORE MATH

The image below is a color exercise by Josef Albers. It includes **parallel** lines and **perpendicular** lines.

1. Look at the three yellow bars. Are these bars parallel or perpendicular to each other? Explain your reasoning.

2. Look at the green, purple, and red bars. Are these bars parallel or perpendicular to the yellow bars? Explain your reasoning.

Rudolf Bauer

Like most painters, Rudolf Bauer experimented with many styles of art. But in abstract art, he found his home. Like Kandinsky, Bauer's art was inspired by music. His paintings are like joyful songs. Bauer even gave many of his pieces musical titles.

Furioso 9 by Rudolf Bauer

Bauer dedicated his life to art. In the 1930s, he opened a museum in Germany. The museum featured his paintings, as well as those of Kandinsky. A racist political group called the Nazis did not approve of the museum. They shut it down and sold his paintings. The ones they didn't sell, they destroyed. Soon after, the Nazis sent Bauer to prison. Despite being in jail, he continued to work. After several months, he was released. Unfortunately, we will never see the great pieces that were destroyed.

Bauer's art has been described as more sculptural than Kandinsky's. This means that his art appears more three-dimensional. But in many ways, he and Kandinsky were alike. They both felt that colors could be used to express feelings and ideas.

LET'S EXPLORE MATH

This painting by Rudolf Bauer includes two triangles. Compare the properties of the triangles. How are they similar? How are they different?

Rounds and Triangles by Rudolf Bauer

Sophie Taeuber-Arp

Sophie Taeuber-Arp was an important voice of early abstract art. She was born in 1889 in Switzerland. Switzerland was a country that valued free expression. For this reason, artists gathered there to pursue their craft. Taeuber-Arp quickly became part of a wild art movement. It was called Dada.

Dada Head by Sophie Taeuber-Arp

Sophie Taeuber-Arp poses behind *Dada Head*.

LET'S EXPLORE MATH

This painting by Sophie Taeuber-Arp has many shapes. Compare the properties of *Quadrilateral A* and *Quadrilateral B*. How are they similar? How are they different?

Quadrilateral A

Quadrilateral B

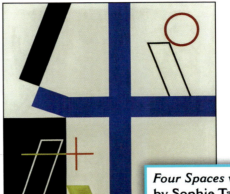

Four Spaces with a Broken Cross by Sophie Taeuber-Arp

The Dada movement was a reaction to World War I. Many artists were shocked by the violence. So instead, Dadaists (dah-dah-ists) embraced silliness. They believed that art should be playful. They thought most artists were too serious. Dadaists created many kinds of art. Most of them were very strange. They made toilet sculptures. They painted a mustache on the *Mona Lisa*. Nothing was off-limits!

Taeuber-Arp was an original even among a wild bunch of artists. She was more than a painter. She was a sculptor, dancer, and puppet maker. Her works speak of freedom and joy. Each piece was created by chance and the mood of the moment.

Blue Poles by Jackson Pollock

Jackson Pollock works in his studio in 1949.

Beyond Geometric Abstraction

The first abstract artists worked primarily with geometric shapes. But, as time passed, artists kept exploring. They wanted to try new techniques. They wanted to create other kinds of abstract art. These artists left behind lines and rays. They focused on more fluid art pieces.

Jackson Pollock

One cannot talk about abstract art without mentioning Jackson Pollock. Pollock was an American. He was born in Wyoming in 1912. As a young adult, he moved to New York. There, he began his life in art. Upon graduating from art school, Pollock struggled with money. It was the era of the Great Depression. Jobs were scarce. But eventually, Pollock found work and advanced as an artist.

Pollock was not a gentle painter. He did not create his works carefully. Instead, he poured paint right onto his canvas. He threw and splattered paint, often with his canvas on the ground. Over time, this technique became known as action painting. Pollock inspired the next generation of abstract artists.

Helen Frankenthaler

Born in 1928, Helen Frankenthaler grew up in New York and was raised in a wealthy family. She began painting at a young age. As an abstract artist, she used Pollock's painting techniques. Setting the canvas on the ground, she poured paint from above.

Although Pollock influenced Frankenthaler, his style was quite different. Pollock covered his paintings in layers of paint. He stacked colors on top of colors. Frankenthaler tried something new. She stained her canvases. In her pieces, paint and canvas became one.

Helen Frankenthaler with her paintings

Mountains and Sea by Helen Frankenthaler

Frankenthaler painted her first canvas using this style in 1952. She created the stains by thinning oil paints. Then, she let the canvas soak up the paint. She named her piece *Mountains and Sea*.

Many people did not understand the painting. They thought it looked unfinished. They thought more work needed to be done. But, her artwork became important. Many artists were influenced by her distinct style. She contributed greatly to the world of abstract art.

The Next Generation

Abstract art does not represent objects from our world. But, it does represent our feelings and ideas. Today, people around the world are creating meaningful abstract art, even young people like you!

Aelita Andre is one such artist. She started painting as a toddler. Some people have called her a child **prodigy**. Over the course of her career, she has created many pieces. Her paintings are filled with vibrant colors.

Andre's art has been compared to the works of Pollock. Like Pollock, she paints wildly. Andre often uses her hands to smear the paint. She also drizzles paint onto the canvas from above. She builds her art color by color. Each painting is a unique masterpiece.

When asked about her artwork she said, "When I do my paintings, I feel free. I don't feel locked up in a tiny world. I just feel free and amazing." She is an inspiration to young artists everywhere!

Aelita Andre

Aelita Andre created this collection of artwork at the age of three.

Aelita Andre artwork from a 2014 exhibit at a New York City gallery.

 Problem Solving

Have you ever wanted to create your own abstract masterpiece? Well, here's your chance!

It's your turn to create your own abstract art. Be sure to include everything on the checklist. (Remember, you can always add more than what is on the list.) Then, answer the questions about your work of art.

1. What is the title of your artwork? What inspired you to choose this title?

2. Choose two shapes from your artwork. Compare the properties of the shapes. How are they similar? How are they different?

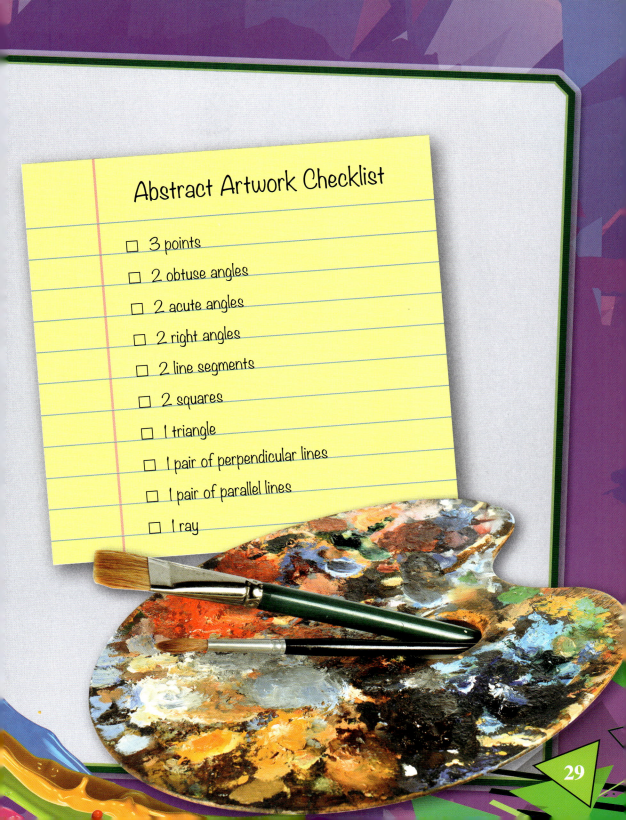

Abstract Artwork Checklist

- ☐ 3 points
- ☐ 2 obtuse angles
- ☐ 2 acute angles
- ☐ 2 right angles
- ☐ 2 line segments
- ☐ 2 squares
- ☐ 1 triangle
- ☐ 1 pair of perpendicular lines
- ☐ 1 pair of parallel lines
- ☐ 1 ray

Glossary

abstract art—a style of art that uses colors and lines to create a drawing that does not look realistic

acute—less than 90 degrees

equilateral—describes a triangle with three equal sides and three equal angles

evolved—changed or developed slowly

isosceles—describes a triangle with two equal sides and two equal angles

line segments—parts of a line between two end points

lines—straight paths of points that continue without end in both directions

obtuse—greater than 90 degrees but less than 180 degrees

parallel—extending in the same direction and the same distance apart, but not touching at any point

perpendicular—intersecting to form a 90-degree angle

perspective—a way of showing depth or distance in a painting or drawing

points—particular positions, locations, or places

prodigy—a young person with extraordinary talent

rays—parts of a line that have one end point and continue on without end in one direction

right—measuring exactly 90°

scalene—describes a triangle with no equal sides or angles

Index

acute angles, 13

Albers, Josef, 5, 10, 16–17

Andre, Aelita, 26–27

Bauer, Rudolf, 10, 18–19

Bauhaus, 17

Braque, Georges, 9

cubism, 9

Dada, 20–21

Frankenthaler, Helen, 24–25

impressionism, 8

Kandinsky, Wassily, 5, 10–14, 17–19

Klint, Hilma af, 10, 14–15

lines, 5, 9, 11–12, 17, 23

Monet, Claude, 8

obtuse angles, 13

op art, 16

parallel lines, 17

perpendicular lines, 17

Picasso, Pablo, 9

points, 11

Pollock, Jackson, 22–23, 26

rays, 11, 23

right angle, 12

Sanzio, Raphael, 7

square, 9, 17

Taeuber-Arp, Sophie, 5, 10, 20–21

triangle, 9, 13, 19

Answer Key

Let's Explore Math

page 11:

Answers will vary, but should include examples of points, lines, rays, and line segments within the artwork.

page 13:

1. Answers will vary, but should describe angles that are less than 90° as acute, angles that are greater than 90° as obtuse, and angles that are equal to 90° as right.
2. Equilateral triangles have 3 equal sides and 3 equal angles. Isosceles triangles have 2 equal sides and 2 equal angles. Scalene triangles have no equal sides or angles.

page 17:

1. Parallel; Parallel lines are two lines that are the same distance apart and do not touch at any point.
2. Perpendicular; Perpendicular lines intersect to form a right angle (90°).

page 19:

Similar—The yellow and black triangles both have 3 sides, 3 angles, and 2 acute angles. Different—The yellow triangle has 3 acute angles and the black triangle has an obtuse angle.

page 21:

Similar—Quadrilaterals A and B both have 4 sides, 4 angles, opposite sides equal in length, and opposite angles equal. Different—Quadrilateral A has 4 right angles and Quadrilateral B has 2 acute angles and 2 obtuse angles.

Problem Solving

Drawings will vary, but everything on the checklist should be labeled in the artwork.

1. Answers will vary, but should include a title and reasoning for choosing that title.
2. Answers will vary, but should describe how the attributes of two shapes in the artwork are similar and different.